SCHOLASTIC

Making Word Walls Work

by Judy Lynch

NEW YORK · TORONTO · LONDON · AUCKLAND · SYDNEY · **Teaching** *Resources*
MEXICO CITY · NEW DELHI · HONG KONG · BUENOS AIRES

Dedication

To my dear friend Bev Ruby. You have given countless precious children
the gift of literacy, and me the gift of unconditional love.

And to my teaching buddies who have *taught me* while we teamed up together
in the classroom and did Reading Recovery at Madison School:

Carolyn Richards, Frances Bigler, and Bonnie Miller: You put out the
welcome mat to kindergarten that has become a magic carpet.

Lisa Niva: Even though you moved two states away, our hearts
will always be one with the first graders we shared.

Denae Merten: You were the first to say, "Sure! Let's teach
second grade together." Thanks for the memories!

Acknowledgments

To Lori Oczkus, who told this first-grade teacher years ago that I needed to write a book.
I laughed in disbelief but you planted the seed of possibility in me.

To the Placer Area Reading Council, the California Reading Association, and affiliates of the
International Reading Association around the world. The people I met, the conferences we attended
and planned, the professional books we read, and the countless opportunities to be with people
passionate about literacy changed my teaching career and life.

To Joanna Davis-Swing, my editor at Scholastic. You are such a treasured professional and
such a sweetheart, too. Our bicoastal relationship is saved by the miracle of e-mail.

To my grown children, Shannon, Kevin, and Michael. Only one left in college—whew!
I treasure being your mom and appreciate the books you tell me I need to read now.

To my husband, Mike. You always have a book in your hand, by the bed, or in your truck!
Thanks for being proud of me because I sure am proud of you!

Scholastic Inc. grants teachers permission to photocopy the reproducible poems and activity pages in this book.
No other part of this publication may be reproduced in whole or in part, or stored in a retrieval system, or
transmitted in any form or by any means, electronic, mechanical, photocopying, recording, or otherwise,
without written permission of the publisher. For information regarding permission,
write to Scholastic Teaching Resources, 557 Broadway, New York, NY 10012.

Cover design by James Sarfati

Interior design by Sydney Wright

ISBN: 0-439-58854-5

Copyright © 2005 by Judy Lynch

Published by Scholastic Inc.

All rights reserved.

Printed in the U.S.A.

3 4 5 6 7 8 9 10   40   13 12 11 10 09 08 07

Contents

Introduction

Why Another Word Wall Book?

Word walls have become a fixture in many primary classrooms. First made popular by Patricia Cunningham's book *Phonics They Use*, word walls have taken off, and books are now available for every kind of word wall imaginable: names, ABC words, word patterns, parts of speech, theme words, and so on. I've written this book to take teachers back to the basic word wall for high-frequency words. My goal is to make this easy! I have surely made many mistakes over the last ten years when constructing word walls, choosing words, and attempting to practice the words efficiently. I hope reading the Dos and Don'ts of Word Walls brings smiles, and even a few chuckles, as you recognize mistakes that you, too, have made. But most of all, I hope the easy suggestions offered in this book help make word walls an effortless, simple part of your literacy program.

Effortless? Simple? Sounds great, but *how*? This book will give you everything you need to set up your word wall and use it all year long. In the back of the book you'll find appendices with word wall words on blackline masters ready to copy for the year. I have carefully chosen these words for primary students rather than simply gathered the most common words used in *all* writing. You'll find a section for kindergarten, first-grade, and second-grade words, and all were chosen for their high utility in general, and in particular for their appropriateness for each grade's reading and writing level.

In the past, I spent countless hours hand-printing my word wall words with a thick black marker onto index cards or sentence strips. But, I've implemented a great time-saver. I have the words on my computer, ready to print each year on colored card stock. With this book, you'll have them ready to copy, too.

The pages in the appendices are color-coded so that if you copy the pages on the suggested card stock, you won't have the same color repeat in a letter box. Within the *Aa* letter box, for example, each word will be printed on a different color card stock. This makes for easy reference to that word throughout the year. I've taken the time to coordinate all this so you don't have to. Before you start, simply take the appendices to a copy store and have them copied on the color of card stock listed at the bottom of each page. And that's it—your words are ready to be introduced and put on your word wall as you need them throughout the year. This will be a big improvement over commercially prepared word wall products, which often provide very small words or words all in the same color. Now, you can have an easily read, boldly colored wall!

Are Word Walls for Reading or Writing?

I have seen teachers and programs emphasize one or the other, but I believe we need to emphasize both. In this book, I will show you an effortless progression from the introduction of new words to a review of the previous week's words to reading and writing the word wall words, and moving the words into independent word centers. This routine works well with kindergarteners, first graders, and second graders and assures us that this important piece of our spelling and reading instruction is thoroughly and systematically taught.

Teaching Word Wall Words With the Word Solvers Tool Kit

I am very excited to introduce here a further element to teaching with word walls that uses the words on your word wall to practice developmental word-learning strategies. In my second book (*Word Learning, Word Making, Word Sorting: 50 Lessons for Success*, Scholastic, 2002), I introduced the Word Solvers Tool Kit. These six strategies for tackling unknown words move K–2 students way past "sound it out." In Chapter 4, I will show you how to use your word wall words to teach and practice these advanced decoding strategies. Every opportunity we give students to problem solve unknown words moves them to independence.

The Dos and Don'ts of Word Walls

We have Patricia Cunningham to thank for getting us started on word walls and for giving us some ground rules to make them effective. I have compiled these into a list of word wall dos and don'ts. I have committed many of the "don'ts" over the years, so don't feel guilty if you have, too! I have added my own explanations under each suggestion.

WORD WALLS

DO:	DON'T:
start with a blank wall. The wall is a teaching tool throughout the year.	**put up all words at once.** The words are added as they are taught.
add five words per <u>week</u>. We want to stress quality, not quantity.	**stress quantity.** For K–1 you may do fewer words per week.
limit total to 110–120 words.	**clutter with too many words.** Have you seen word walls so cluttered that the words were not easily visible?
finish adding by April 15.	**forget to still practice daily.** We practice daily even after all the words have been added.
use high-frequency words.	**use theme words here.** *Pilgrim* and *polliwog* are appropriate with a topic of study. Put them on a chart elsewhere.
use different colored paper. The words in each letter box should be on different colors for easy practice. The appendices have this done for you with words large enough to see.	**put the same colors together.**
practice daily. Build it into a daily 10–15 minute routine and the students won't let you forget.	**put up and forget.**
<u>DO</u> A WORD WALL! Many people HAVE a word wall up in their room. This book will give you a simple, systematic plan to DO it!	**<u>HAVE</u> A WORD WALL!**

Adapted from Patricia Cunningham

Chapter 1

Prepare Your Classroom

*T*eachers have way too much to do before school starts. This chapter is designed to make your word wall preparation easy and efficient. You will find choices for word wall configurations, practice books for daily use, and sample word lists and word walls for your grade level. Let's get started!

Below are the steps in detail to prepare your room:

❶ Construct your word wall.

❷ Make simple word practice booklets.

❸ Look over your word list and sample word wall.

❹ Copy word lists (see Appendices B–D).

❺ Look through books and poetry for word wall words.

Construct Your Word Wall

❖ Choose the largest, most visible space available for your word wall. Is it easy to see from everywhere in your classroom?

❖ Choose a background color that will not distract from the colorful words you will put up later. I once put up a sunny yellow background that looked great until the words went up and everything became a blur. Now, I like to achieve the maximum contrast by using light or dark blue, white, or black.

❖ Once you've chosen the color, quickly staple sheets of the butcher paper to the wall. A border can cover uneven edges later.

Divide Your Word Wall Into Letter Boxes

Teachers are busy, and measuring for a word wall is usually not high on our to-do list To keep this procedure simple, I put up word walls with an even number of boxes across and down. I divide the total space in half and the center point becomes the middle of the word wall. Further equal divisions create equal spaces, so there is no need for complex measurements. Four boxes across and six down are good for a vertical space. Six boxes across and four down are good for a more horizontal space. I use yarn as dividers, pinning up strands first with pushpins and then stapling the finished lines.

Aa	Bb	Cc	Dd	Ee	Ff
Gg	Hh	Ii	Jj	Kk	Ll
Mm	Nn	Oo	Pp	Qq	Rr
Ss	Tt	Uu	Vv	Ww	Xx Yy Zz

▲ *horizontal word wall*

Aa	Bb	Cc	Dd
Ee	Ff	Gg	Hh
Ii	Jj	Kk	Ll
Mm	Nn	Oo	Pp
Qq	Rr	Ss	Tt
Uu	Vv	Ww	Xx Yy Zz

▲ *vertical word wall*

Aa	Bb	Cc	Dd	Ee
Ff	Gg	Hh	Ii	Jj Kk
Ll	Mm	Nn	Oo	Pp Qq Rr
Ss	Tt	Uu Vv	Ww	Xx Yy Zz

▲ *limited space word wall*

Do you have limited space? You can make a twenty-box word wall and combine little-used letters in the same box. Another solution to a small space is to "retire" word wall words that have been up for months and that most students are regularly spelling correctly. Take these words down with great fanfare and remind your students that they are expected to spell them correctly from now on. Students who need to see a few of these key words can be given 8½- by 11-inch copies of your grade-level word wall (pages 13–18) to keep in their writing folder.

Put Alphabet Letters in the Boxes

For years I handwrote alphabet letters, but now I create them on my computer so they are bold and easy to see from anywhere in the room. You'll find ready-to-reproduce letter cards in Appendix A. If you have a very large room, you may wish to enlarge them.

Border Your Word Wall

I choose a simple border that does not visually compete with the words I will put up on the word wall throughout the year.

Make Simple Word Practice Books

Practicing writing word wall words every day takes a lot of paper. I don't want to waste time passing it out, so I make My Word Book booklets for each of my students. These are *not* dictionary word reference books. They are booklets with many blank spaces to practice writing word wall words as a whole group, in small groups, and in independent centers. I run the covers (page 9) on construction paper so they are inexpensive to make with regular school materials. I choose a color different from the reading journals and writer's workshop journals we also use. For example, our reading journals have a yellow cover, our writing journals have a white cover, and our My Word Book booklets have a light-blue cover. I run off many pages of the word boxes (page 10), front to back. Then I have student helpers (bless those fifth and sixth graders!) staple them together. These booklets usually last at least half the year.

Pages for My Word Book booklets

On page 10, you'll find a reproducible page which you can use to make word practice books for your students. Run these pages front to back. About twenty pages, stapled with a simple cover, will last each student many months for all the word work you do. For handwriting reference, the top of the box is for tall letters and the bottom is the baseline. I emphasize good handwriting as we practice. If you have an overhead projector, make several overheads of this page.

Look Over Your Word List and Sample Word Wall

We want our kindergarteners, first graders, and second graders to use these common words for fluent reading and writing. From a list of the twenty most common words used for writing (Sitton) and reading (Eeds, 1985), over half are on the kindergarten list and all are on the first-grade list in this book. You can rest assured that the key words primary students need to know are here. I carefully chose from some of the best-recognized lists available for high-frequency words: those by Sitton, Fry, Gentry, and Shefelbine. I had to choose carefully because, except for Gentry's, the other widely used lists reflect "the most common words in English" (Fry, 1993). In other words, most lists are for *all* ages. However, the needs of emergent readers and writers are unique. So the key words are all here, but are often reordered by priority for K–2 students.

Kindergarten Words

For kindergarteners, I have chosen the words they use to read and write. On most frequency word lists, *I* is not even in the top twenty, but *with* is! Yet we know every 5-, 6-, and 7-year-old starts most sentences with the word *I*. The word *like* is number 66 on one popular list many schools use. But if we wait that long to teach it, our students will practice writing "I lick pizza" and "I lic Jessica" until they form a habit we need to break later. So, the kindergarten list includes high-utility words such as *mom, dad, see, like, can,* and *is*. All of these twenty words are important to kindergarten writing and reading. You should teach them in the order that makes the most sense, based on their relevance to your shared reading, writing, or literature-based basal program. Soon our kindergartners will write and read the patterned sentences they naturally start out with:

I like ___.   I see ___.   I can ___.   Mom is ___.
Dad can see ___.   You have ___.

My Word Book

by

First-Grade Words

It's a good idea to start first graders with a review of the kindergarten words. Words learned before summer can easily slip away. The twenty kindergarten words will give students a firm footing in the repetitive books most first graders start with. The review list will also fit perfectly with the patterned writing most first graders use early in the year.

The next eighty new words for first grade are appropriate for the reading and writing they'll do. Of course, I included *play*, even though it is number 367 on one popular list. I did not put *oil* on the list (number 88 elsewhere). I have been doing writer's workshop with 5-, 6-, and 7-year-olds since 1984, and I assure you, oil is not a hot topic. Friends and family are, however, so I have included *friend* and *family* on the list. I have added *because* to the list for writing purposes. When writing in response to a book in guided reading ("Why was Mrs. Wishy Washy mad?"), we teach first graders to turn the question around and use *because* in the middle of the answer ("Mrs. Wishy Washy was mad *because* the animals got in the mud.").

The first-grade words may strike you as short and simple, but many of the most common words are not phonetic (*the, was, come, said*) so don't be deceived. These words will give you numerous opportunities to teach irregular words and complex vowel and consonant patterns.

Second-Grade Words

When I teach second grade, I pretest my students using the first-grade list. Ideally, during the second week of school I test them on 25 words each day. I learned to give them paper that is already numbered 1–25, since asking new second graders to number their papers from 1 to 25 can take forever!

Looking at their papers, I analyze how many students are missing each word by putting tally marks on a master copy. When I see *thay, sed, frist, frum, uther* and so on, I know which words are still a problem, and I plan my review

accordingly. The first-grade words are the bedrock on which to build. When you look at the second-grade list, you will notice that it consists of longer and more challenging words. The list will give you many opportunities to teach spelling and decoding strategies for complex words that are still high utility for this grade level.

Copy Word Lists

The words in Appendices B, C, and D contain black-line masters for each grade level. I have followed Patricia Cunningham's excellent advice and color-coded the pages at the bottom so that when you copy them according to these instructions, each word within each letter box will be a different color. This strategy makes it easy to access the words during practice and review ("I'm looking at the letter *Ll*. The word is yellow. It is . . ."). Take the appendix for your grade level to a copy store and have the pages printed on card stock in the color suggested at bottom. Or, you can purchase the card stock and print the words yourself on your copy machine at school. I have chosen ten colors commonly found in card stock:

Light Blue	pastel blue
Medium Blue	sometimes called "Lunar Blue"
Yellow	pastel yellow, sometimes called "Canary Yellow"
Gold	deeper yellow, sometimes called "Sunburst Yellow"
Pink	pastel pink
Hot Pink	deep pink, sometimes called "Fireball Fuchsia"
Orange	sometimes called "Cosmic Orange"
Red	sometimes called "Rocket Red"
Green	pastel green
Lime	sometimes called "Terra Green"

If one of these colors isn't available, simply substitute another color you like. Just be sure that you're consistent and that you copy all the pages that are coded with the color for which you're substituting.

Kindergarten teachers have five pages to copy, which will cost about a dollar. First- and second-grade teachers have 25 pages to copy, which will run about five dollars. But once you've copied the words, you are ready for the whole year, which certainly beats hand-printing new words each Friday after school. Once copied, I cut up the brightly colored words and put them in alphabetical order. I keep them in a folder with a master list of all the words so I can check them off as I teach them. You'll come to love the brightly colored, boldly printed words on your word wall.

Look Through Books and Poetry for Word Wall Words

Now that your words are ready, which words should you teach first? It depends on your curriculum and materials. Keep in mind that the lists in this book are in alphabetical order and I have only included words that are frequently used by primary students. *You* will choose the order in which to teach your grade-level list, based on the materials you are already using. Look at the words that are in those early poems, basal readers, or literature you already have, and let them guide you. If you have a spelling program that emphasizes word patterns, you can incorporate word wall words that have the same pattern that week. Are you seeing *there* and *their* misused or misspelled in children's writing? I would teach these homonyms together, then put them on the word wall and review them as long as necessary. The important thing is that the whole list of words is taught and reviewed thoroughly by the end of the year.

Kindergarten

I use *Brown Bear, Brown Bear, What Do You See?* by Bill Martin, Jr., for kindergarteners. The repetitive "What do **you see**?" and "**I see a** . . ." are perfect for links to *I, you, a,* and *see.* Big books and simple poetry are perfect for finding more connections to the word list. I have included here "Baa, Baa, Black Sheep," which contains *have, you, the,* and *and.* I also like to use the word list to build oral language with these words. Speaking in complete sentences builds a base for English structure that helps later reading and writing. I model these sentence patterns orally and encourage students to repeat them and add their own endings. For example, I might say, "I like to eat chicken. Who can tell me what they like to eat?" Students love to respond and I have them use the complete sentence in their answer: "I like to eat ___."

Here are some other sentences for which students can fill in the blanks:

You can see a ___.   A ____ is big.

I can go to___.   I see ____(color) ____(object).

I have a ___ (pet, toy).

Baa, Baa, Black Sheep

Baa, baa, black sheep,
Have you any wool?
Yes sir, yes sir,
Three bags full;
One for the master,
One for the dame,
And one for the little boy
Who lives down the lane.

Kindergarten Word Wall Words

a   and   at   can

dad   have   he   I

in   is   it   like

love   mom   of   see

she   the   to   you

Aa a and at	**Bb**	**Cc** can	**Dd** dad	**Ee**	**Ff**
Gg	**Hh** have he	**Ii** I in is it	**Jj**	**Kk**	**Ll** like love
Mm mom	**Nn**	**Oo** of	**Pp**	**Qq**	**Rr**
Ss see she	**Tt** the to	**Uu**	**Vv**	**Ww**	**Xx** **Yy** you **Zz**

▲ Sample Finished Kindergarten Word Wall (You can add your own students' names.)

First-Grade Word Wall Words

1. a	26. friend	51. love	76. so
2. all	27. from	52. make	77. some
3. an	28. get	53. man	78. than
4. and	29. go	54. may	79. that
5. are	30. good	55. me	80. the
6. as	31. had	56. mom	81. them
7. at	32. has	57. my	82. then
8. be	33. have	58. nice	83. they
9. because	34. he	59. no	84. this
10. but	35. her	60. not	85. to
11. by	36. here	61. now	86. too
12. came	37. him	62. of	87. two
13. can	38. his	63. on	88. up
14. come	39. how	64. one	89. us
15. dad	40. I	65. or	90. very
16. day	41. if	66. other	91. was
17. did	42. in	67. out	92. we
18. do	43. is	68. over	93. went
19. down	44. it	69. play	94. were
20. each	45. its	70. put	95. what
21. eat	46. jump	71. read	96. when
22. family	47. know	72. said	97. who
23. find	48. like	73. saw	98. will
24. first	49. little	74. see	99. with
25. for	50. look	75. she	100. you

Aa	Bb	Cc	Dd	Ee	Ff
a	be	came	dad	each	family friend
all	because	can	day	eat	find from
an	but	come	did		first
and are	by		do		for
as at			down		

Gg	Hh	Ii	Jj	Kk	Ll
get	had here	I is	jump	know	like
go	has him	if it			little
good	have his	in its			look
	he how				love
	her				

Mm	Nn	Oo	Pp	Qq	Rr
make me	nice	of other	play		read
man mom	no	on out	put		
may my	not	one over			
	now	or			

Ss	Tt	Uu	Vv	Ww	Xx Yy Zz
said so	than they	up	very	was when	Xx
saw some	that this	us		we who	Yy you
see	the to			went will	Zz
she	them too			were with	
	then two			what	

▲ Sample of a completed first-grade word wall (includes 20 review kindergarten words + 80 new words)

Second-Grade Word Wall Words

1. about	26. few	51. must	76. started
2. after	27. food	52. name	77. take
3. again	28. found	53. never	78. their
4. along	29. give	54. new	79. there
5. also	30. going	55. next	80. these
6. another	31. got	56. night	81. things
7. any	32. great	57. number	82. those
8. around	33. home	58. off	83. thought
9 asked	34. house	59. often	84. three
10. away	35. important	60. old	85. through
11. back	36. into	61. only	86. together
12. been	37. just	62. our	87. under
13. below	38. keep	63. own	88. until
14. best	39. large	64. part	89. use
15. both	40. last	65. people	90. want
16 brother	41. left	66. place	91. way
17. called	42. line	67. right	92. well
18. children	43. long	68. same	93. where
19. could	44. made	69. say	94. which
20. didn't	45. many	70. school	95. why
21. different	46. might	71. should	96. words
22. does	47. more	72. show	97. world
23. don't	48. most	73. sister	98. would
24. every	49. mother	74. small	99. write
25. father	50. much	75. something	100. your

Aa	Bb	Cc	Dd	Ee	Ff
about another	back brother	called	didn't	every	father
after any	been	children	different		few
again around	below	could	does		food
along asked	best		don't		found
also away	both				

Gg	Hh	Ii	Jj	Kk	Ll
give	home	important	just	keep	large
going	house	into			last
got					left
great					line
					long

Mm	Nn	Oo	Pp	Qq	Rr
made most	name next	off only	part		right
many mother	never night	often our	people		
might much	new number	old own	place		
more must					

Ss	Tt	Uu	Vv	Ww	Xx
same sister	take those	under		want why	
say small	their thought	until		way words	Yy your
school something	there three	use		well world	
should started	these through			where would	Zz
show	things together			which write	

▲ Sample of a completed second-grade word wall (These words should be put on the word wall slowly over time.)

First Grade

What poetry, big books, and literature-based basal are you using? Let this guide you in choosing which words to teach. I look for teaching points using the word wall words to support the curriculum and materials I already have. Some possible teaching connections:

Short-Vowel Patterns:
short a: **an**, m**an**, th**an**, **and**, **at**, d**ad**, h**ad**
short e: th**en**, wh**en**, w**ent**
short i: d**id**, w**ill**, **in**, **it**
short o: n**ot**
short u: j**ump**

The rime pattern is a key decoding strategy for chunking words (for more on chunking, see page 34). In a rime, the pattern not only sounds the same but is spelled the same. *Fought* and *taught* rhyme, for instance, but they are spelled differently and are therefore not rimes. After the first consonant(s), if there are any, the vowel and consonants make a pattern (rime) in every syllable in English. I have bolded them to make them easy to identify.

Silent-*e* Patterns: are, came, come, have, here, like, love, make, nice, one, some, were (Note that many are not regular!)

Second Grade

What poetry, Big Books, and literature-based basal are you using? Let this guide you in choosing which words to teach. I look for teaching points using the word wall words to support the curriculum and materials I already have. Some possible teaching connections:

Vowel Sounds
With r: after, another, brother, different, every, father, large, more, mother, never, number, part, sister, started, under, where, words, world

Multisyllabic
Words: another, different, important, something, together

▲ *Independent work*

Vowel Patterns: ab**ou**t, **a**g**ai**n, **a**r**ou**nd, **away**, c**ou**ld, d**ee**p, f**ew**, f**oo**d, f**ou**nd, gr**ea**t, h**ou**se, m**igh**t, n**ew**, n**igh**t, **ou**r, **ow**n, r**igh**t, sh**ou**ld, sh**ow**, th**ou**ght, thr**ough**, w**ou**ld, y**ou**r

Songs are yet another text in which to find word wall words. Following is my version of an old song that first and second graders love. It's a great review of first-grade words (*me, out, to, my, little, with, friend, some, and, I, if, it, a, for, they*) and a teaching tool for second-grade words (*take, don't, old*). I put the song on sentence strips in the pocket chart and have students find the words. When they know it well, I give them their own copy and have them highlight the word wall words with a highlighter pen or yellow crayon.

Take me out to my little league game,
Take me out with my friends.

Buy me some nachos and soda pop,
I don't care if it ever ends.

With a cheer, cheer, cheer for my team,
If they don't win it's a shame.

For it's 1, 2, 3 strikes you're out,
At the old ball game.

Chapter 2

Systematic Practice with Word Wall Words

*T*eaching and practicing words is the heart and soul of using the word wall in my classroom. I have found that systematic practice, ten to twenty minutes each day, provides multiple opportunities for my students to master word wall words for reading and writing. I also like the structure that this practice gives my students— and me. When my students come in from their afternoon recess, they know it's word practice time, and they automatically take out their word wall booklets.

In this chapter I'll describe a three-week sequence that you can repeat over and over throughout the entire year. I'll show you what to do during each of these weeks to build up a steady word wall practice.

How to Implement Systematic Classroom Practice

Below I describe the entire three-week sequence, which you can use with your students throughout the year. It includes the introduction of new words each week, a review of the previous week's words, and ongoing independent practice in word centers. Since kindergarteners learn fewer words, the process can be shortened and simplified for them. The following system works well for me, but feel free to adapt it to fit your class's needs. Let's look at what to do each week.

Week #1

Introduction of New Words

Monday (Time: 5 minutes for kindergarten, 10–15 minutes for first and second grades)

1 Present New Words

With second graders, I present five new words a week. With first graders, I start with two to three new words a week and build up to five. With kindergarteners, for much of the year I present only one word per week, and then increase to two words during the last few months of the year. (This presentation of new words can be modified as needed for kindergarteners.) I present the new word thoroughly on Monday and Tuesday and look for examples in the books we're reading. I also encourage students to write the words in their writing journals.

❖ I sit at my overhead (or use the chalkboard) and present the first new word.

❖ This activity gives me an opportunity to talk about any special features of the word or any tricky parts.

❖ I write the word for children to see, saying each letter and emphasizing correct letter formation.

2 Student Response: Clap It   Slap It   Snap It

❖ I vary the response for chanting the spelling of the word to provide suspense and variety.

I say: "Ready . . ." (Pencils are all down, hands up at shoulder level.)
"Clap it." (Students look at the new word on the screen or board while chanting the spelling and clapping for each letter.)
or
"Slap it." (Students look at the new word on the screen or board while chanting the spelling and slapping their legs for each letter.)
or
"Snap it." (Students look at the new word on the screen or board while chanting the spelling and snapping their fingers for each letter.)
Then we say the word together with a cheer.

3 I say: "Write it!"

The whole class writes the word in their My Word Book booklets. As they write it, they softly say the spelling, putting it more deeply into their memories. I check on students quickly, giving help where needed.

What have we done with this word? We've seen it, said it, heard it, and felt it. Repeat this activity with the week's other new words.

Review of New Words

Tuesday (Time: 5 minutes for kindergarten, 10–15 minutes for first and second grades)

Repeat the process from the day before, but this time, present the words in a different order. For kindergartners with whom you're working on just one word, simply run through the process as you did on Monday.

Teachers everywhere have developed ingenious ways to chant the letters of words and add movement. Some clap high over the head for tall letters, down low for letters that go under the line (g, j, q, y), and right in the middle for most letters. One Midwestern teacher told me that during basketball season her class pretends to dribble the ball as they say each letter, and pretend to shoot a basket as they say the word at the end. Keep it fun, fast-paced, and focused.

Review of *All* Word Wall Words

Wednesday–Friday
(Time: 5 minutes for kindergarten, 10–15 minutes for first and second grades)

On Wednesday, add the new words to the classroom word wall with great fanfare. The continued review of all the word wall words is crucial if your students are going to be able to use these words in their reading and writing. The number of words I review each day varies. Some days we're really clicking along, and then there are days when individual students need help (or redirection!) or everybody needs help on a difficult word. I skip around, choosing new words to review in my allotted time each day. But I will come back to a particularly challenging word over and over until students really "get" it.

Remember, review of your word wall words is crucial. Years ago, I was pleased to "have" a word wall up in my room. The words were put on the word wall and I expected my students to use them thereafter. Since then I've learned not to assume *anything*! If I want to see the words used correctly in writing, or read effortlessly in reading, then I must support those expectations with continued practice.

Following are steps for reviewing the words on your word wall.

① Read the Word Wall Words

(Time: 1–2 minutes for kindergarten, 3–5 minutes for first and second grades)

Before I ask children to write words from the word wall, we spend a few minutes reading them. Always be sure to focus the group's attention quickly on a word. For example, you might say, "I'm looking at the letter *Ww*. The word is gold . . ." I always follow this basic pattern, first saying the letter of the box the word is in, followed by the color of the word card. Again, you can see the benefit of having each word in a letter box on a different color of card stock—it makes the words much easier to spot.

Sometimes students may need additional direction to get their eyes quickly to a letter box. In those cases, I give a few basic directions to help them find the area where the letter box will be—for example, "I'm looking in the top row" or "I'm looking down the left side of the word

TIP: Here are two quick ways to **read** the words that include a pause for think time:

Laser Pointer

Buy an inexpensive laser pointer at an office supply store. (Note: Keep it out of the reach of children. They should not look into the light. I keep mine up high on the top ledge of my whiteboard.) Direct students' eyes to a letter box as described above. Focus the laser light on the word to read. Give them a little think time. When the light goes off, the class reads the word in unison.

Pointer Tap

Use any long pointer you already have: a yardstick, a dowel, or a long Big Book pointer. Direct children's eyes to the letter box as described above. Instruct them to think of the word as you touch it with the end of the pointer. When you then tap the word, the class reads the word in unison.

wall." These directions help students who might be having trouble focusing on the sea of letters and words before them. Once their eyes are in the right vicinity, I mention the letter box that they should zoom in on. The goal is to quickly get their eyes to the letter box and the words in it that I want to practice.

Repeat this basic pattern for each word you review for reading from the word wall:

- **Locate the word.**
- **Read it!**

② Write the Word Wall Words

(Time: 3–4 minutes for kindergarten, 7–10 minutes for first and second grades)

After you've spent a few minutes reading some words on the word wall, it's time to *write* words for a few more minutes. I choose words that students need to practice writing— sometimes these are the words they have just read, and sometimes they are entirely new words. I repeat the procedure I used for teaching the new words on Monday and Tuesday. I have found that simplicity leads to better learning.

❖ **Locate the word on the word wall:** Follow the same procedure you used when reading the words, above: "I'm looking at the letter *Cc*. The word is pink. It is . . ." The basic pattern is always the letter name, then the word's color.

❖ **Students respond:** Students read the word in unison. Make sure all eyes are on the correct word.

❖ **I say: "Ready . . ."** (Pencils are all down, hands up at shoulder level.)
"**Clap it.**" (Students look at the word on the word wall while chanting the spelling and clapping for each letter.) *or*
"**Slap it.**" (Students look at the word on the word wall while chanting the spelling and slapping their legs for each letter.) *or*

"**Snap it.**" (Students look at the word on the word wall while chanting the spelling and snapping their fingers for each letter.)

Then we say the word together with a cheer and . . .

❖ **I say: "Write it!"**
The whole class writes the word in their My Word Book booklets As they write it, they softly say the letters to put the spelling more deeply into their memories. I check on students quickly, giving help where needed. They are to drop their pencils and put their hands up in ready position as soon as they finish writing the word. This speedy response keeps the whole process quick and focused.

Repeat this basic pattern for each word you review for spelling and writing from the word wall:

❖ **Locate the word.**
❖ **Read it.**
❖ **Clap, slap, or snap it.**
❖ **Write it!**

Week #2

Each week I follow the routine outlined above. On Monday and Tuesday, we work on new words. Wednesday through Friday, we review the words by reading and writing from the word wall. But I have added a twist to reviewing the previous week's words *in addition to* simply practicing off the word wall. After the first week of school, when we have a few words we can review, we play Memory Match, a Concentration-like game, with the words from the previous week. This builds in continued review of the prior week's words. You can continue playing this Concentration game throughout the year. Simply put the previous week's words into Memory Match each Monday to keep up the review.

▲ *Memory Match*

Memory Match

Materials

- pocket chart (I use a small one and mount it in my calendar area.)
- 10–12 word cards—5 words from the previous week, with duplicates of each (You may wish to add a sixth word pair; choose any word wall word that could use some extra review.)
- 10–12 number cards—index cards numbered 1–10 (or 1–12) to hide the word cards for review (Colored index cards work best so children can't see the word underneath.)

Preparation

1. Make 12 number cards that will last the whole year. I use colored index cards and write a number, 1–12, in heavy black marker on each.

2. Each week, make two sets of the previous week's new word wall words. I use a black marker to write each word on two white index cards.

3. Put numbered cards in your pocket chart in rows.

4. Hide the word cards randomly behind the number cards. After each complete game, I "secretly" reshuffle the cards so students can't memorize cards' positions.

How to Play

- Call on one student to choose a number.
- Reveal the word behind the number.
- The whole class reads the word in unison.
- Call on another student to pick the second number.
- Reveal the word behind the number.
- The whole class reads the word in unison.

Is it a match? If so leave the words uncovered and continue with more student tries. If not, cover the words back with their numbers and continue with more student tries.

When to Play

In my classroom, any time we gather on the rug by our calendar we can play Memory Match for a few minutes. Students who normally dawdle instead of sitting down hurry to get in their place so they can participate. I start calling on students who are ready when about three-fourths of the class has assembled. Nobody wants to miss the game. Play for as long as you have time. You may only reveal one or two matches or continue until all the words are matched.

Updated Flash Card Practice

Another way to continue practicing reading the words from the previous week is to do an updated version of traditional flash card practice. This version includes a pause for students before they respond. If we don't allow for a group "think time," a few quick students will shout out the answer, causing the others to lose out on processing time. Using the previous week's words, or a cumulative pile, flash one word at a time:

- **Point to your head.** Students copy you, pointing to their temple to convey thinking.

- **Point to the group.** Students read the word in unison.

- **Repeat.**

Week #3

Independent Practice in Word Centers

On the third week of the cycle, the new words from Week #1 are placed in independent word centers, thus adding another key component of learning word wall words. Remember:

Week #1 Introduce the new words and put them on the big word wall in the middle of the week.

Week #2 Play Memory Match. Use two index cards for each word from the previous week in a Concentration game.

Now we come to . . .

Week #3 Independent Word Centers. The words that were new two weeks ago now go into centers where students practice the word wall words cumulatively the rest of the year.

And that's the system!

❖ It provides the **structure** that students need. It gives them routines they can expect, and no time is wasted.

❖ It provides the **variety** that keeps students engaged. You can vary the clap it, slap it, snap it responses to keep children alert.

❖ It's **easy**, allowing you to plan your word work lessons and independent work with a method in mind.

❖ It includes **regular** reading and writing of the high-frequency words students need to know.

❖ It's **focused** and **fun**!

In Chapter 3 I'll give you ideas for eight word centers to take you through the entire year.

Updated Flash Card Practice

Independent
Word Wall Centers

*T*he primary way we can help our students master high-frequency
words is by giving them practice—and lots of it. We call attention
to the words in big books, poetry, and small books used for instructional
groups in guided reading. In writing, we model using the words in shared
writing and then pass the pen to students who can spell the word on
chart paper for interactive writing. The best "spelling test" is when
students spell the words correctly in their own writing in natural contexts
like journals, writer's workshop, and a thank-you note to Grandma.

Using the Words in Independent Centers

Word centers can provide independent practice of the words you have taught (during Week #1) and reviewed in Memory Match (during Week #2). The third week, I move the words from Memory Match into two centers. Recall that we made two index cards for each word wall word in order to play Memory Match. Now those cards can go into two separate centers: Rainbow Writing and Mix-It Fix-It, where students can continue the review on their own.

A word about independent centers. I have found that teacher modeling and student practice under teacher supervision provide for independence sooner rather than later in the year. Time spent at the beginning of the school year showing the procedures and expectations for each word center pays off when students become independent workers. When my class is actively, quietly, and productively working in these centers, I can pull reading groups for small-group reading instruction. Of course, students do not automatically become active, quiet, and productive independent workers all by themselves. Model and practice high standards in these areas before asking students to demonstrate these behaviors on their own.

Following are ideas for eight independent word centers.

① Rainbow Writing

Materials
- word cards—3-by-5-inch cards made the week before for use in Memory Match. Take one of each word card and add them to the cumulative pile for practice.
- crayons
- students' My Word Book booklets, or scratch paper
- a small container to hold 3-by-5-inch index cards

Center Directions:

1. Pick a word wall word to copy and five crayons.

2. Write the word in one color, and whisper the letters as you write them.

3 Repeat over the top of each letter in four other colors.

NOTE: Make sure children write the entire word with the same color and then choose another color to write it in again, tracing over the word. They should *not* write each letter in a different color; if children stop after each letter to choose another crayon they break the flow of whispering the letters as they write them. Children should also not decorate the words with artistic flourishes. Such embellishments turn the activity into an art project when the goal is simply to write the same word five times to create a "rainbow" of colors for each letter.

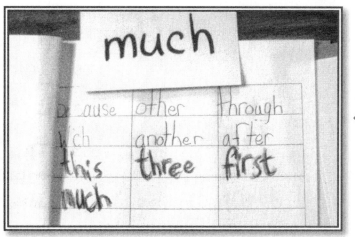

◀ *Rainbow Writing*

② Mix-It Fix-It

Materials

- word cards—3-by-5-inch cards made the week before for use in Memory Match
- magnetic letters—2–4 of each letter; I like to put them on a magnetic surface that's easy for students to reach, such as the side of a file cabinet.
- container, such as a small plastic basket, to hold the cards as they accumulate over the year (If you want to hold the cards on the magnetic surface, purchase "pencil/comb" holders sold in the fall for high school students' lockers. They have a magnetic backing and hold 3-by-5-inch cards efficiently.)
- My Word Book booklets, or scratch paper
- pencils

Center Directions:

1. Pick a word wall word card.
2. Make the word with magnetic letters.
3. Mix up the letters.
4. Fix the word by putting the letters in order.
5. Write the word in your word wall book.
6. Start over!

TIP: When I'm working with kindergartners or early first graders, I like to have the words already placed on small magnetic trays (burner covers from the housewares department at your local store or small cookie sheets work well). With one word on each tray, children do not have to search for letters to build the word. To introduce this to any grade, I first model the process and then let them practice. I have them whisper the letters as they build the word and as they write the word.

③ Reading the Word Wall

Materials

- class word wall
- long pointers, such as yardsticks or dowels

Center Directions:

1. Pick a long pointer.
2. Pick a letter box to practice.
3. Touch words on the word wall with the tip of the pointer.
4. Read each word softly as you touch it.
5. Repeat with a new letter box.

④ Word Detectives

Materials

- word wall words on index cards (you can use the words from Rainbow Writing or Mix-It Fix-It)
- My Word Book booklets
- pencils
- Big Books and poems to find word wall words
- highlighter tape (removable and reusable from teacher's stores or catalogues such as 1-800-ART-READ)

Center Directions:

1. Take a word wall card and one piece of highlighter tape.
2. Search for the word in big books and poems.
3. Tape the word when you find it and record in your My Word Book booklet.
4. Peel off the tape and look for the word in other books and poems.
5. Repeat with a new word card.

▲ Word Detectives

Independent Chunking Centers: Word Wall Words With Common Chunks and Rimes

The next four centers involve "chunking." For a description of word chunks, and how I explain them to students, see my discussion on page 34.

⑤ Egg-citement

Materials

- plastic eggs found in the spring
- large permanent marker
- rime list from page 26
- basket to hold the eggs
- My Word Book booklets, or scratch paper

Preparation

✱ To prepare each egg, hold the egg so that the round (fat) end is to the left. Write a rime pattern on the other, narrower end (on the right), putting the vowel close to the middle of the egg. (For example, one egg could have -og, another egg -ack, and so on until you have the patterns you want your students to practice in a center.)

✱ On the round end of the egg, write beginning consonants, which, when joined with the rime pattern on the narrow end, will form words (see figure below, left). Be sure to write the letters close to where the egg halves join so that a word will clearly be formed when the egg is rotated. (For example, f, d, l, and h join with -og to make fog, dog, log, and hog.) When your students are ready for a challenge, use blends and digraphs as the beginning consonants to form more complex words (shack, crack, track, black, and so on).

Center Directions:

1. Take one egg at a time.

2. Twist the egg in opposite directions.

3. Write down each word as it is made.

4. Can you think of more words using this pattern?

⑥ Flip Books

Materials

- 4-by-6-inch index cards or card stock
- list of common chunk/rime patterns (or follow the patterns taught in your spelling/phonics/basal program)

Preparation

✱ To make blank books:

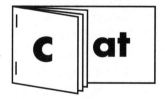

1. For each book, take several cards and cut all but one of them in half, lengthwise (into 3-inch pieces).

2. Leave the bottom card full size (6 inches) and write the chosen rime pattern on it, to the right-hand side of the card (for example, -at, -ug, or -op).

3. Write different onsets (beginning consonants) on each of the half-size cards. The number will depend on the number of words you want to make with the word pattern.

4. Staple the half-size cards to the left side of the bottom card. When flipped, they should create words to read and write (see figure on page 29). Possible words for your flip book include:

cat	**f**at	or for a challenge	**spl**at	**ch**at	**br**at
bug	**r**ug		**sl**ug	**ch**ug	**sn**ug
lop	**t**op		**cr**op	**fl**op	**dr**op

Grade Level Guidelines:

Kindergarten: Choose short vowel patterns children have learned.

First Grade: Make sure short-vowel patterns are well understood, then move to long-vowel patterns.

Second Grade: Review short vowels and then move on to more complex long-vowel patterns.

Center Directions:

1. Pick a flip book.

2. Write the top word in your *My Word Book* booklet.

3. Flip the top letter card and use the new letters to make a new word.

4. Repeat, until you have flipped all top letters.

5. Can you add your own words?

⑦ Word Race

Materials
• My Word Book booklets, or scratch paper
• pencils
• 3-minute egg timer
• *The Scholastic Rhyming Dictionary* by Sue Young, or other rhyming dictionary

Center Directions:

1. Take a word chunk the teacher has given you to practice.

2. Turn the timer over.

3. Write down as many words with that chunk as you can think of.

4. When the time runs out, draw a line on your paper.

5. Next, look up the pattern in the rhyming dictionary and copy all the words you didn't think of yourself.

⑧ Grocery Chunks*

Materials
• empty packages from food and other store items (for example, Cracker Jacks, Slice, Tide, Shake 'n Bake, Slim Jim) that children have brought in
• My Word Book booklets, or scratch paper
• pencils and crayons

Preparation

✳ Gather empty packages that children have brought in. Looking at the words on the packages, find the chunks and then quickly brainstorm orally with the class to see if each pattern generates enough words to justify putting the package in the center. *Milk*, for example, only generates *silk* and *bilk*. *Crest*, on the other hand, generates *best*, *rest*, *test*, *chest*, *nest*, *pest*, *vest*, and therefore works well for this activity.

✳ Display the words on a bulletin board or in a binder in a plastic sleeve.

Center Directions:

1. Choose a grocery item to make words.

2. Write the word at the top of your booklet.

3. Write as many words as you can think of with that chunk.

4. Underline the chunk each time with a crayon.

* The idea of Grocery Chunks is adapted from Patricia Cunningham, who says she shops with an eye for common patterns now.

Chapter 4

Using the Word Wall to Teach the Word Solvers Tool Kit

*I*n my second book, Word Learning, Word Making, Word Sorting: 50 Lessons for Success (Scholastic, 2002), I showed teachers how to give students a Word Solvers Tool Kit. This kit has six prompts that coach students to look more and more deeply into words they don't know. When decoding a word, these prompts take students way beyond "sound it out" and leads them to strategies that are consistent with the ways they naturally learn words. When children are first learning to read, they notice the beginning and ending sounds of words before they pay attention to the detail within a word. The tool kit builds self-confidence in beginning readers because it gives them strategies to tackle unknown words while reading.

TOOL	FOCUS
Get My Mouth Ready	Initial letters in a word
Look Across the Word	Final letters and suffixes
What Do I Know?	Analogy (known to new)
Chunk the Word	Rime Pattern/Larger Parts
Look Into the Word	Embedded Letters/Clusters/ Multisyllables
What Other Sound Can I Try?	Flexibility with Vowel and Consonant Variations

Teaching the Tool Kit With Word Wall Words

I usually like to teach these tools in the context of stories in guided reading or Big Books. But I have also found it very useful to use the tool kit when teaching or reviewing word wall words. In this chapter I'll show how I do that and give you some sample words to use with your class. The chart above shows the six tools and the decoding focus for each.

> Enlarge the Word Solvers Tool Kit reproducible on page 33 and post it in your classroom. I like to put colored clothespins in front of the tools as I teach them to my students. After reading, ask "Which tool did you use?"

Get My Mouth Ready

This is an early tool for emergent readers. When children start reading, many of the words they read are based on a repetitive pattern, picture clues, or known sight words. The next step for them is to start matching what they say with the printed words on the page—instead of inventing words that match the pictures. Get My Mouth

Ready teaches children to use the beginning letters to decode unknown words. "Get your mouth ready" is a prompt I learned in my Reading Recovery training more than ten years ago. I adapted it here because all the prompts for this tool kit are written as "self-talk." I want to coach students to tell themselves what to do when they don't know a word. A first step for kindergarteners and first graders (or any student ignoring the print) is to look at the beginning letters and form those sounds in their mouth. Often this oral/aural technique triggers the unknown word. It teaches them that they must look at print. The rest of the tool kit will take them further into words and word parts.

With Kindergarteners

Kindergarteners often learn their letters and sounds but don't know what to do with them in reading. Using their known word wall words can show them how to differentiate between words. Early on, when teaching the first words (*I, see, like, can,* for example), we learn to look at the first letter and get our mouths ready. They learn that *I, s, l,* and *c* make different sounds when we get our mouths ready—and therefore signify different words.

Other word wall words to contrast beginning letters: *dad, he, mom, you.*

Word Solvers Tool Kit

Super Reader

* **Get my mouth ready.**
* **Look across the word.**
* **What do I know?**
* **Chunk the word.**
* **Look into the word.**
* **What other sound can I try?**

With First Graders
Good word wall words to contrast beginning
sounds: his/this   go/no/so   me/he/be/she

With Second Graders
A quick review of this tool is all second graders,
should need. Some word wall words to use:
brother   should   things   might/night/right

Look Across the Word

Get My Mouth Ready is a tool that only begins
to train emerging readers to look at print in
detail. Very soon after they start using the first
letters effectively, we need to move them on to
other parts of words. Developmentally, they
next attend to the ending letters and suffixes
(*-ing, -ed, -er*) in a word. To encourage this next
strategy, I teach them the next tool: Look Across
the Word. In order to get children to take in the
whole word, we have to model with our eyes—
or perhaps a finger—the way we move from the
beginning to the end of a word. How else will
they ever read *mom, mommy,* or *mother* correctly?
There are many examples from our word wall
words to ensure they don't get stuck on the
beginning of a word.

Kindergarten
in/is/it   have/he   like/love   a/and/at
to/the   see/she

First Grade
than/that them/then   her/here   the/they

Second Grade
much/must   home/house   same/say
another/any   been/best   food/found

What Do I Know?

This is a very powerful tool in reading that
allows students to tackle unknown words that
would have paralyzed them before. The goal
here is to teach them to think by *analogy*—
taking something known to figure out something
new. Successful readers will look for any word
part they know or that is similar to something
they know. I always burst a prominent

misconception when I tell my students that I
can't possibly teach them all of the words in
books. But, I *can* teach them how to figure out
words they don't know, which is just as good.
They learn to look for any part they know
(*sh-, -ing*) to use in taking a word apart
(*sh-out-ing*). Analogy also encourages them to
look for similarities (*our/out*) and to give a new
word a try. The attempts children make when
using What Do I Know? are not always perfect—
you may, for example, get *fat-her* for *fa-ther*—
but I encourage them to try and listen to see if
the word makes sense (meaning) and sounds
right (structure). When students are reading to
make sense, the tool What Do I Know? becomes
a powerful ally.

   Kindergarteners usually use only the first
two tools in the tool kit. If, however, you have
some students who are ready for this, use the
first-grade words with them. Once I teach this
tool in first and second grade, I introduce ALL
new word wall words with this tool. I do not
read the word to them—I expect them to look at
the new word and ask themselves, "What do I
know?" Following are some word wall words to
use as you teach and review this tool. Each one
contains a part children might know that will
help them read the entire word.

First Grade
has   **that**   **fri**end   **nice**   **little**   **fam**ily
go/no/so   **for**

Second Grade
something   another   important   things
into   started

Chunk the Word

I explain "chunks" to students by comparing
the concept to chocolate. I put out both hands,
palms up, and ask them to imagine a little bit
of chocolate in one hand and a big chunk in
the other. "Which one do you want?" I ask.
Of course, they all point to the imaginary big
chunk. I then explain that their brains want big
chunks, too—not of candy but of letters. In the

purest sense, a chunk is a rime pattern like those in the charts below. As teachers we have called them phonograms and used them to generate word families (-ack: back, stack, backpack). They share a common pronunciation and are spelled the same, unlike rhyming words, which can contain different spellings to produce the same sound (taught and fought).

The bigger goal for me is to have my students look at larger units of print to decode unknown words. Many of these common patterns are found in the word wall words you are teaching. From the charts below, I have chosen common patterns found in the first- and second-grade word wall lists used in this book. When you teach one of these words, its usefulness compounds as students see the many words they can read and write with the same pattern. You can also teach the same pattern together (an, than, can, man, or might, night, right).

▲ Chunk the Word

Kindergarten* and First-Grade Word Wall Words With Common Chunks/Rimes

Chunk/Rime	Word	Chunk/Rime	Word	Chunk/Rime	Word
-ad	had	-en	when	-or	for, or
-ake	make	-end	friend	-ot	not
-all	all	-ent	went	-ow/ou	how, out
-an	an, **can**, man, than	-et	get	-ump	jump
-and	**and**	-id	did		
-are	are	-ill	will		
-at	**at**, that	-im	him		
-ave	**have**	**-in**	**in**		
-aw	saw	-ind	find		
-ay	may, play	**-it**	**it**, little		

* Common chunks/rimes in kindergarten word wall words are in **boldface**.

Second-Grade Word Wall Words With Common Chunks/Rimes

Chunk/Rime	Word	Chunk/Rime	Word	Chunk/Rime	Word
-ace	place	-ell	well	-ore	more
-ack	back	-en	children, often	-ot	got
-ade	made	-ew	few, new	-ow/o	below, own, show
-ake	take	-ight	might, night, right		also
		-im	important	-ow/ou	about, around, found, our
-all	called, small	-in	into	-um	number
-ame	name, same	-ine	line	-un	under, until
-an	another, any, many	-ing	going, something, things		
-ar	started	-ive	give		
-ay	away, say, way	-old	old		
-ed	asked, called	-ong	along, long		

Common Chunks/Rimes

Wylie and Durrell (1970) discovered that these 37 phonograms are found in almost 500 primary-grade words:

-ack	**-ail**	**-ain**	**-ake**	**-ale**	**-ame**
-an	**-ank**	**-ap**	**-ash**	**-at**	**-ate**
-aw	**-ay**	**-eat**	**-ell**	**-est**	**-ice**
-ick	**-ide**	**-ight**	**-ill**	**-in**	**-ine**
-ing	**-ink**	**-ip**	**-it**	**-ock**	**-oke**
-op	**-ore**	**-ot**	**-uck**	**-ug**	**-ump**
-unk					

Next-Highest Utility Chunks

After the highest 37, these are the 52 next most common patterns:

-ab	**-ace**	**-ad**	**-ade**	**-ag**	**-all**
-am	**-amp**	**-and**	**-ane**	**-ang**	**-ar**
-are	**-ark**	**-ave**	**-eak**	**-eal**	**-ear**
-ed	**-eed**	**-eep**	**-eet**	**-en**	**-end**
-ent	**-et**	**-ew**	**-id**	**-ig**	**-im**
-ime	**-ind**	**-int**	**-ive**	**-ob**	**-od**
-og	**-old**	**-one**	**-ong**	**-ope**	**-orn**
-ow/o	**-ow/ou**	**-ub**	**-uff**	**-um**	**-un**
-ung	**-ush**	**-ut**			

We want our students to know that the slowest, least effective way to decode a word is letter by letter, sound by sound. By chunking text, we tap into how the brain naturally works, chunking information. Could any of us remember our Social Security number if it wasn't chunked into three sets? Following are some word wall words to teach or review this tool for first and second graders.

First Grade

| an/can/man/than | day/may/play | at/that |

Or take these word wall words (the first word in each row, shown in boldface), to brainstorm many more with this common rime pattern:

-ad: **dad**, bad, clad, fad, grad, lad, mad, pad, sad

-ake: **make**, bake, brake, cake, fake, flake, Jake, lake, quake, rake, shake, snake, take, wake

-all: **all**, ball, call, fall, gall, hall, mall, small, stall, tall, wall

-an: **an**, ban, bran, can, clan, fan, man, pan, plan, ran, scan, span, tan, than, van

-and: **and**, band, bland, brand, gland, grand, hand, land, sand, stand, strand

-at: **at**, bat, brat, cat, chat, fat, flat, gnat, hat, mat, pat, rat, sat, spat, splat, that, vat

-aw: **saw**, claw, draw, flaw, gnaw, jaw, law, paw, raw, saw, straw, thaw

-ay: **may**, bay, bray, clay, day, gray, hay, lay, pay, play, pray, ray, say, spray, stay, way

-en: **when**, Ben, den, hen, men, pen, ten, then, yen

-end: **friend**, bend, blend, lend, mend, send, spend, tend, trend

-ent: **went**, bent, cent, dent, gent, rent, scent, sent, spent, tent, vent

-et: **get**, bet, fret, jet, met, net, pet, set, vet, wet, yet

-id: **did**, bid, grid, hid, kid, lid, rid, Sid, skid, slid, squid

-ill: **will**, bill, chill, dill, drill, fill, frill, gill, grill, hill, kill, mill, pill, skill, spill, thrill, will

-im: **him**, brim, dim, grim, him, Jim, Kim, prim, rim, skim, slim, swim, Tim, trim, whim

-in: **in**, bin, chin, din, fin, grin, kin, pin, shin, sin, skin, spin, thin, tin, twin, win

-ind: **find**, bind, blind, grind, kind, mind, rind, wind

-it: **it**, bit, fit, flit, grit, hit, kit, knit, lit, little, pit, quit, sit, skit, slit, spit, split, wit

-or: **or**, for, nor; **with silent *e*:** bore, chore, core, more, pore, score, shore, snore, store, wore

-ot: **not**, blot, clot, cot, dot, got, hot, jot, lot, plot, pot, rot, shot, slot, spot, tot

-ow/ou: **out**, bout, clout, pout, rout, scout, shout, snout, spout, sprout, stout, trout

how, bow, brow, chow, cow, now, plow, pow, vow, wow

-ump: **jump**, bump, chump, clump, dump, grump, hump, lump, plump, pump, stump, thump

Second Grade

Second graders need to see the chunks in multisyllabic words to effectively tackle more complex texts in reading. Use the following word wall words (the first word in each row, shown in boldface) to provide practice and review of the fourth tool in the tool kit, Chunk the Word. This also provides vocabulary practice when we define and explain the words we are taking apart.

-ace:	**place**, birthplace, deface, disgrace, embrace, fireplace, misplace, replace, shoelace, unlace
-ack:	**back**, attack, backpack, crackerjack, haystack, racetrack, sidetrack, thumbtack
-ade:	**made**, arcade, blockade, charade, crusade, decade, homemade, invade, lemonade, parade
-ake:	**take**, cupcake, earthquake, milkshake, mistake, pancake, rattlesnake, snowflake
-all:	**called**, baseball, birdcall, football, install, meatball, pitfall, rainfall, recall, small
-ame:	**name**, became, inflame, nickname, overcame, same
-an:	**another**, any, Batman, began, caveman, dustpan, Japan, many, outran, suntan, Superman
-ar:	**started**, ajar, all-star, boxcar, guitar, handlebar, streetcar, superstar, Zanzibar
-ay:	**away**, birthday, decay, display, hallway, highway, okay, railway, say, way, yesterday
-ell:	**well**, doorbell, eggshell, farewell, misspell, nutshell, retell, unwell
-en:	**children**, amen, bullpen, often, open, pigpen, playpen
-ew:	**few**, anew, brand-new, cashew, curfew, new, outgrew, screw, threw, withdrew
-ight:	**might**, daylight, delight, flashlight, midnight, night, right, sunlight, tonight, uptight
-im:	**important**, brim, grim, imagination, immediate, impossible, prim, skim, swim, whim
-in:	**into**, begin, drive-in, hairpin, Rumpelstilskin, sheepskin, tailspin, violin, within
-ine:	**line**, airline, canine, clothesline, combine, define, outline, recline, sunshine, valentine
-ing:	**going**, earring, everything, offspring, plaything, shoestring, something, things
-ive:	**give; long-*i* sound:** arrive, beehive, contrive, deprive, nosedive, revive, skydive, survive
-old:	**old**, behold, billfold, blindfold, enrolled, household, retold, threshold, untold, withhold
-ong:	**along**, belong, dingdong, headstrong, lifelong, long, oblong, prolong, wrong
-ore:	**more**, adore, before, drugstore, encore, explore, folklore, ignore, outscore, restore
-ot:	**got**, apricot, cannot, flowerpot, forgot, jackpot, mascot, robot, slingshot, snapshot, teapot
-ow/o:	**below**, **own**, aglow, outgrow, overflow, rainbow, scarecrow, show, undertow
	ago, buffalo, dynamo, hello, Idaho, info, Mexico, pueblo, yo-yo
-ou:	**about**, around, found, our
-um:	**number**, chrysanthemum, eardrum, humdrum, plum, scum, strum
-un:	**under**, begun, homespun, outrun, unimportant, unimpressed, unthinkable, until

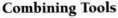

Combining Tools

Effective readers combine tools to tackle unknown words. Using What Do I Know? and Chunk the Word together is even more powerful than either strategy alone. When children combine these strategies, they learn to look for chunks they know in large words they never thought they could read. The words on page 38 should provide ample practice that they can apply to text.

Look Into the Word

This tool is vital because we have so many similar words in English (*father/farther, shirt/short*). When students are using beginning and ending letters consistently, it is time to have them pay attention to the details within a word. We want them to look at the letters embedded in words, vowel clusters, and multisyllabic words. Below are some word wall words to use when teaching or reviewing this tool with first and second graders.

First Grade

came/come	dad/did
like/love	than/then

Or take a word wall word (the first word in each pair) and show how a change in the middle makes a new word:

but/bat/bet/bit	him/ham/hem/hum
make/made	man/men
some/same	

Second Grade

home/house	most/must
their/there	there/three
words/world	

Or take a word wall word (the first word in each pair) and show how a change in the middle makes a new word:

below/bestow	brother/bother
children/chicken	don't/didn't
father/farther	found/friend
mother/matter	same/some

sister/sinister	started/strutted
thought/taught	where/were

When our students use this tool, they learn to look!

What Other Sound Can I Try?

It would be so much easier to teach students to read and write in Spanish or Russian. Why? Because these are phonetic languages that have a regular sound/symbol match. English, on the other hand, is rich in variations and multiple sounds for the same letter. That is why this tool, which teaches flexibility with sounds, is needed for effective reading. Too many times I have seen students read a word that doesn't make sense and then give up. Often, the problem is that they are mispronouncing the word because they are using the wrong vowel or consonant sound. This tool teaches them to try again and look at alternative sounds for letters in the problem word. In the end, the word should make sense *and* look right. Here are some word wall words to teach or review this tool.

First Grade

w**as**/**u**s	ni**c**e/**c**an	**all**/**at**/day
come/**like**/we**re**	**u**p/p**u**t	**kn**ow/**n**ot

Or take a word wall word (the first word in each pair) and show how sounds can change:

at/**ate**	**can**/**cane**	**do**/**go** **u**s/**u**se
fr**om**/**ph**one	s**ai**d/s**e**t	

Second Grade

about/**a**gain/**a**long/**a**way	**o**ff/**o**ld/an**o**ther
our/sh**ou**ld/th**ou**ght	l**i**ne/g**i**ve

Or take a word wall word (the first word in each pair) and show how sounds can change:

b**oth**/br**oth**	b**a**ck/b**a**ke	w**or**ld/f**or**
nev**er**/f**ir**st/n**ur**se		

When children use this tool, they learn that if their first try doesn't succeed they can simply try something else!

Bb

Dd

Aa

Cc

Ff

Hh

Ee

Gg

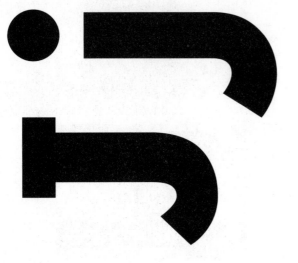

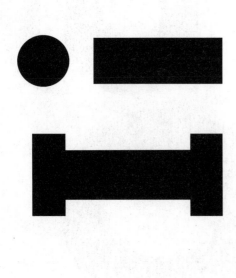

Enlarge and run these letters on white card stock for the letter boxes on your word wall.

Nn

Mm

Oo

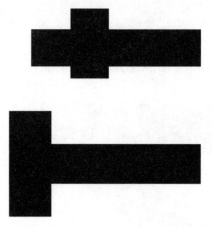

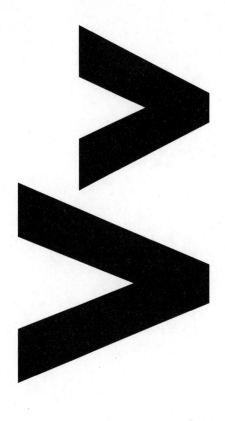

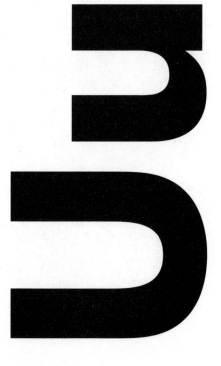

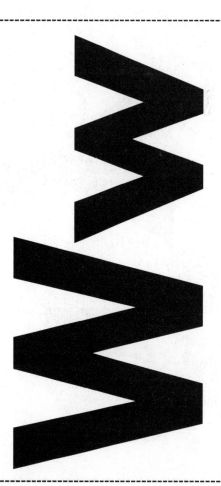

Enlarge and run these letters on white card stock for the letter boxes on your word wall.

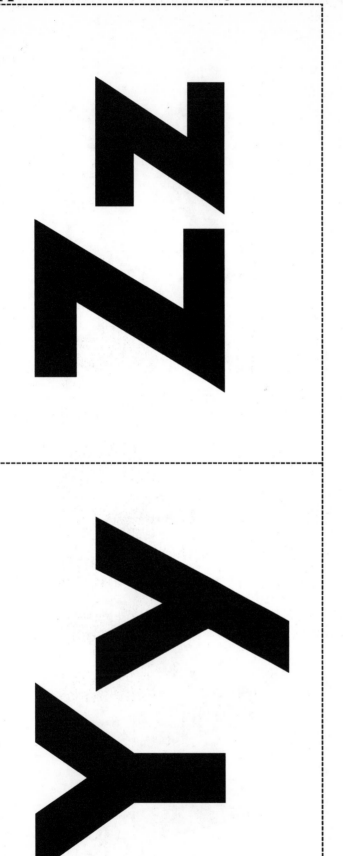

Appendix A

Copy these pages on the color card stock listed at the bottom of each page. Cut out each word around the letters to clearly show the word's shape. Put the words in alphabetical order, and they're ready to go.

Print on light blue card stock / Grades K–1

dad **is**

see

have

he

can

she

I

at love

to you

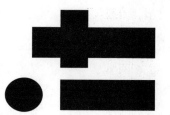

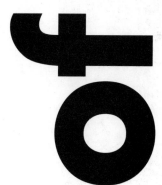

Print on yellow card stock / Grades K–1

The first 20 words are a review of the kindergarten words (see Appendix B). Copy these pages on the color card stock listed at the bottom of each page. Cut out each word around the letters to clearly show the word's shape. Put the words in alphabetical order, and they're ready to go.

because

him

first

may over

went

than

Print on gold card stock / Grade 1

not

then

who

up

Print on green card stock / Grade 1

put

do

man

has

come

as

look

it's

its

nice

read

we

them

Print on hot pink card stock / Grade 1

other

here

good

know

Print on hot pink card stock / Grade 1

with

eat

that

find

Print on light blue card stock / Grade 1

did

us

her

on

came

family

too

all

Print on lime card stock / Grade 1

for

little

but

get

Print on medium blue card stock / Grade 1

two

out

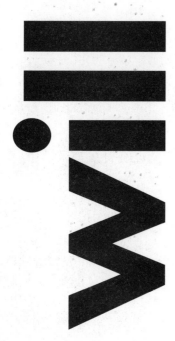

will

so

Print on medium blue card stock / Grade 1

were

play

from

this

Print on orange card stock / Grade 1

how

are

down

friend

Print on pink card stock / Grade 1

when

they

very

some

Print on pink card stock / Grade 1

or

if

now

my

Print on pink card stock / Grade 1

said

jump

was

his

Print on red card stock / Grade 1

one

be

me

day

Print on red card stock / Grade 1

what

had

saw

make

Print on yellow card stock / Grade 1

by

go

each

no

Print on yellow card stock / Grade 1

(Note: For a review of the word wall words for grade 1, see Appendix C.) Copy the pages on the color card stock listed at the bottom of each page. Cut out each word around the letters to clearly show the word's shape. Put the words in alphabetical order, and they're ready to go.

both

different

give

after

Print on gold card stock / Grade 2

found

keep

house

started

Print on gold card stock / Grade 2

there

place

long

would

Print on gold card stock / Grade 2

asked

write

been

those

Print on green card stock / Grade 2

name

only

more

small

Print on green card stock / Grade 2

words

left

three

every

Print on hot pink card stock / Grade 2

away

show

own

much

Print on hot pink card stock / Grade 2

brother

many

does

about

Print on light blue card stock / Grade 2

way

part

something

song

through

Print on light blue card stock / Grade 2

mother

food

any

could

Print on lime card stock / Grade 2

sister

take

into

night

Print on lime card stock / Grade 2

world

going

just

under

must

new

best

these

often

well

say

along

Print on medium blue card stock / Grade 2

called

don't

also

which

never

same

great

made

Print on orange card stock / Grade 2

things

line

old

want

Print on orange card stock / Grade 2

around

home

last

didn't

together

why

most

should

another

got

few

children

Print on red card stock / Grade 2

might

off

large

number

Print on red card stock / Grade 2

thought

use

right

school

Print on red card stock / Grade 2

where

below your

people

important

again

back

father

Print on yellow card stock / Grade 2

their

next our

until

Print on yellow card stock / Grade 2